Beyond The Code

Comprehension and Reasoning Skills

2

Nancy Hall

EDUCATORS PUBLISHING SERVICE
Cambridge and Toronto

Printed in Benton Harbor, MI, in June 2022
ISBN 978-0-8388-2402-3

21 PPG 22

Contents

Review of *Beyond The Code 1*

• Remember the words you learned in *Beyond The Code 1*?
Draw a line from the word to the picture of the word.

eat

see   down

door   call

play   they

tree

Which Words Rhyme?

• Draw a line from the word in the first list to the word that rhymes
in the second list.

keep	more
stay	some
give	mutt
come	sleep
for	may
what	live

More review of *Beyond the Code 1*

• Use the words in the box to finish the sentences below.

with
out
day
have
open
was
says

1. I will go _____ you.

2. We _____ six cats.

3. Mom _____ I must go to bed.

4. If the sun is up, it is _____.

5. Will you _____ the door for me?

6. He _____ sad to miss the bus.

7. My dog yips to go _____.

Words for **Send Plum Back**

1. **now** = **Now** rhymes with .

   We got a flat; **now** we'll have to jog.

   Write and spell it: _____

2. **roll** = r + O + L

   A **roll** is good to eat.   Write and spell it: _____

3. **know** = no

   I **know** how to add.   Write and spell it: _____

   grow = **Grow** rhymes with **know**.

   I have **grown** a lot, but I'll **grow** more.

   Write and spell it: _____

4. **want** = w + on + t

   Do you **want** to come in?

   Write and spell it: _____

5. **ever** = ev + er

   Have you **ever** lost your hat?

   Write and spell it: _____

   never = **Never** rhymes with ever.

   We **never** get to play.    Write and spell it: _____

Read the word list again.

Words for **Send Plum Back**

• Draw a line from each sentence to the picture it goes with.

We have **grown** good crops.

Ben **wants** to see what's in the box.

A ball can **roll** fast down the hill.

Kim will eat **now**.

If I **grow** a bit, the pants will fit.

We have **never ever** had more fun!

Send Plum Back

Britt has a soft, pink pig, a runt she calls Plum. She put up a pig·pen for Plum in a clump of trees by the track. Day in and day out Britt has fed her pig bran and scraps, swill and slops. Britt fills Plum's pan to the rim, and the pig gulps it down. The rest of the day Plum just sits in the sun and rolls in the mud.

Day by day the pig grows more and more plump. In fact, with all this flab and fat, Plum cannot run! Plum's soft skin has grown stiff with mud. Grass and twigs stick to the mud. Plum is a bit of a mess! Now Plum is a full-grown pig and is fit to sell at last! Britt knows Plum is fat and will sell fast.

Britt has spent a lot to get Plum fat so he will sell well. But, to be frank, *now* Britt wants Plum to stay! Still, Plum costs a lot, so Britt can't keep him as a pet.

Britt is glum. She will miss Plum. She can't send him off, but she knows she must! Her dad says Plum must go the next day. Dad tells his men it will be a trick to get Plum in the truck, but they must.

In a wink Britt has a plan! If Plum fled now,
he'd miss the truck and have to stay. So Britt opens the
pen door to let Plum go. But Plum is as big as a blimp
and just lolls in the pen. He can•not run. He will not go!
Britt's plan to let Plum go is a flop! Plum just wants
to stay in the slops. (But Plum can•not know what's
to come!)

Now it's six o'clock, and Britt is snug in bed, but she has not slept well at all. She hears the truck and Plum's grunts. The men have crept up as still as can be. They must be swift to grab Plum. At last they get a grip on the pig and flip him on his back. Plum can't stand up. He's as cross as can be!

Plum grunts and grunts. The men huff and puff. They can't lift Plum. He's as big as a blimp! They fix a strap on the pig and pull him. Then, quick as a wink, they slip Plum into the back of the truck.

Britt didn't see the truck as it went back up the track, and she is just as glad! It's a fact: Plum *had* to go. But it was still sad to send him off as they did. Britt felt bad all day . . . and the next. At last it struck her—she must not be sad. To be frank, Plum *was* a bit of a slob. And (as all pigs do) he did stink just a tad. Still, Plum was the best pig ever!

"Will Britt get one more pig·let?" you ask.
Never!

Yes **No** **Can't Tell**

• Draw the face to show the answer.

1. Was Plum a black pig?

2. Did Britt give Plum a lot to eat?

3. Did Plum smell a bit bad?

4. Can it cost a lot to keep a pig?

5. Did Britt want to sell Plum?

6. Was it a snap to get Plum into the truck?

7. Did Britt hear the clock at six and jump out of bed?

How would you feel if you had to sell Plum?

_____

- -

_____

11

Draw the rest of plump Plum and draw what he eats.

Think About It!

1. Tell one thing that can grunt but is not a pig.

_____

- -

_____

2. Name two things that can smell bad.

_____

- -

_____

3. Name two things you can feed.

_____

- -

_____

4. How are all pigs the same?

_____

- -

_____

5. Why did Britt say Plum was "a bit of a slob?"

_____

- -

_____

6. Tell why Britt will not get one more pig·let.

_____

- -

_____

Can You Figure This Out?

• Write your own answer to each question.

What can you do with:

a ball? _____

       your feet? _____

           your hands? _____

               your pal? _____

What hops? _____

       What can swim? _____

           What can you give a pal? _____

Introduction to **The Camp Out**

• With some drill you can learn to read longer words. Look at the pictures below and then read the word, one part at a time. Now put the two parts together and say the word again.

= riv + er = river

= un + pack = unpack

= back + pack = backpack

= a + sleep = asleep

= rab + bit = rabbit

= hid + den = hidden

= bed + room = bedroom

More Introduction

• Circle the word that is the right answer.

1. If a man robs you,
   is he a **rob** + **ber** or a **rub** + **ber**?

2. Do you want to play on
   May Day or **Sun** + **day**?

3. Will you run fast if you see
   a **mon** + **ster** or a **ham** + **ster**?

4. If you want to go to camp, will your
   Mom say, **"May** + **be"** or **"No way!"**?

5. Will a pal ask you to come
   o + **ver** or **un** + **der**?

6. Do you ask what will
   hab + **it** next or **hap** + **pen** next?

7. Will Tom say he wants to be
   by **him** + **self** or by **her** + **self**?

Words for **The Camp Out**

1. **bear** =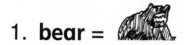

   A **bear** sleeps in a den.   Write and spell it: _____

2. **that** = the + at (**That** rhymes with **cat**.)
   That is my mom.   Write and spell it: _____

3. **make** = **Make** rhymes with .

   Did you **make** that in class?   Write and spell it: _____

   take = **Take** rhymes with **make**.

   They **take** a nap.   Write and spell it: _____

4. **find** = f + I + nd
   Ken **finds** the pin.   Write and spell it: _____

   kind = **Kind** rhymes with **find**.
   What **kind** of dog do you have?

   Write and spell it: _____

5. **fire** =

   The **fire** is hot.   Write and spell it: _____

6. **after** = af + ter
   Wags runs **after** the ball.

   Write and spell it: _____

Now read the word list again.

Words for **The Camp Out**

• Draw a line from each sentence to the picture it goes with.

Sal sees the **bear** cub.

After we get logs, we'll **make** a fire.

Do you want this plum or **that** one?

It was **kind** of you to **find** my lost hat.

Jan **takes** her bag to the bus stop.

The Camp Out

It is a swell day with no fog or mist. Kris begs her dad to go on a camp out. She plans to set up a tent on the bank of the West Bend Riv·er. Kris wants to go so bad, but she knows she can't go by her·self.

At last Dad gives in and tells her, "OK, we'll go! Tell your pal Pam she can come as well!"

Kris jots down a list of all they will have to pack. Dad tells her not to take a lot of stuff. At last they stop by to pick up Pam and then set off to find the best spot to camp.

Kris and Pam spot a plot of flat land. So Dad stops and they dump the stuff. Kris and Pam help Dad till the tent's all set up. The tent is grand. It has a big front flap so they can go in and out. Next to the tent Kris puts up a flag that flaps in the wind.

But Dad says they still have lots of jobs to do. They dig a fire pit and put some rocks down in it. After they un·pack, Dad sends the kids to get sticks for the fire, and he hunts for flint to make the fire go. Next they cram a back·pack with all the stuff they will eat and strap it up in a tree so no bears can get it. At last they come to the end of the tasks.

Now Kris and Pam and Dad tramp down to the riv·er. As they stomp in the mud they spot some tracks. They can see the prints well in the wet mud of the riv·er bed. Dad tells the kids what kind of prints they are. They hunt for more tracks and find elk and skunk prints, fox and rab·bit tracks, as well as a duck!

Back at the tent Dad wants to have a nap, so Pam and Kris go back down by the riv·er to play. By and by they find an old raft hid·den in the grass. They hop on, but as they do it begins to sink. They jump off fast!

Next Pam and Kris jump from rock to rock and try not to fall in. But Kris slips and gets her socks all wet. Brrrr! Now she is cold! "May·be I will go back to the tent," she says at last.

By now it is dusk and the sun has set. Dad sets out to find the kids just as Kris and Pam get back to camp. Dad makes a hot fire for ham and eggs. The kids get out the buns and milk to drink.

As they eat, Kris tells Dad she fell in and got wet. "But it was still a good day," Kris adds.

Dad grins. "I'm glad you had fun. Now off to bed, kids! Hit the sack!" he says.

In a wink Kris and Pam are fast asleep in the tent.

It's just six o'clock as Kris and Dad get up. The sun is up, but not Pam! She stays snug in bed for a bit. Pam is the last to get up.

As they pack up the stuff to go back, Kris asks her dad, "Did you have fun, Dad? *We* had a blast! Wasn't it swell? May·be you will want to camp out next Sun·day as well?"

Yes 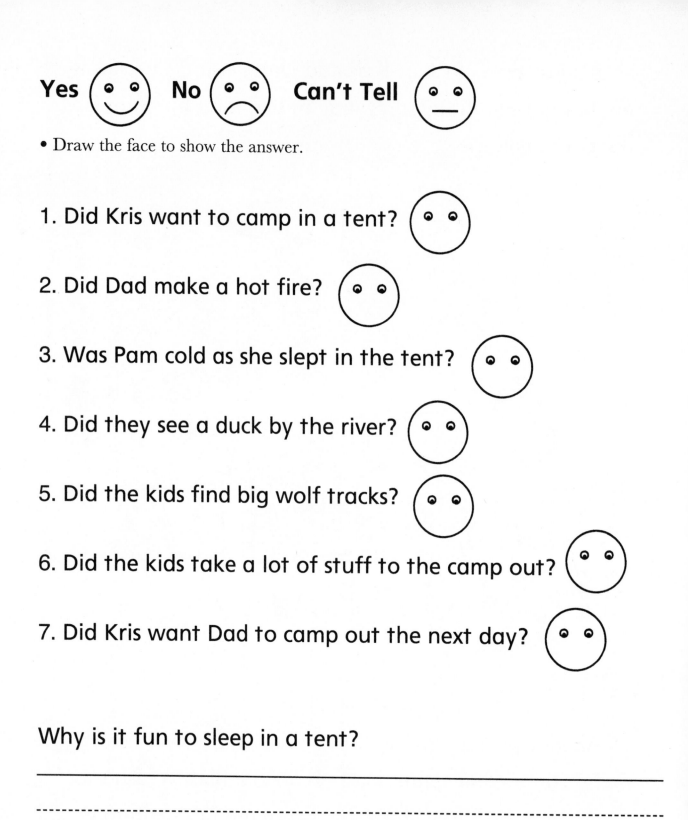 **No** **Can't Tell**

• Draw the face to show the answer.

1. Did Kris want to camp in a tent?

2. Did Dad make a hot fire?

3. Was Pam cold as she slept in the tent?

4. Did they see a duck by the river?

5. Did the kids find big wolf tracks?

6. Did the kids take a lot of stuff to the camp out?

7. Did Kris want Dad to camp out the next day?

Why is it fun to sleep in a tent?

_____

- -

_____

Draw the flap on the tent and put a flag next to it.

Think About It!

1. Name two things that can be a blast.

   _____

   -

   _____

2. How are all tents the same?

   _____

   -

   _____

3. Why did Kris have cold feet?

   _____

   -

   _____

4. Why did Dad tell Kris not to pack a lot of stuff?

   _____

   -

   _____

5. If you see a raft on a riv·er, will you take it a·cross?
   Tell why or why not.

   _____

   -

   _____

6. Would this trip be fun on a cold, damp day?
   Tell why or why not.

   _____

   -

   _____

Can You Figure This Out?

• Find the word on the train that is the best answer
and write it on the line.

1. What has a plug? _____

2. What's fun to eat? _____

3. What makes a flag flap? _____

4. What can you put lots of stuff in? _____

5. What did Kris slip and fall into? _____

6. What can you camp in and stay dry? _____

wind
tent
snack

sink
trunk
river

Introduction to **Greg Can't Sleep**

• Draw a line from the word to the picture of the word.
Some are review words from *Beyond the Code 1*.

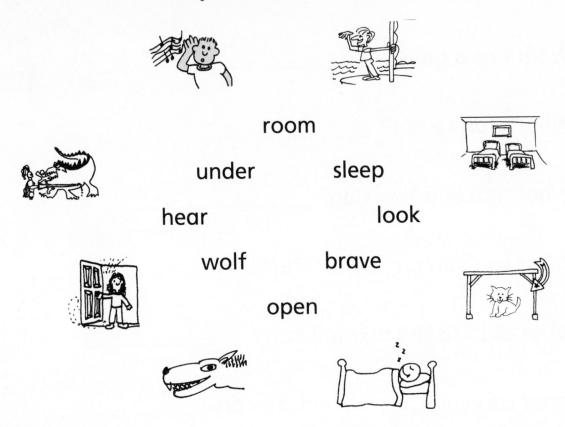

room

under   sleep

hear   look

wolf   brave

open

Which Words Rhyme?

• Draw a line from the word in the first list to the word that rhymes
in the second list.

lamp   stick

blink   pin

hall   rest

quick   drink

pest   all

begin   damp

Words for **Greg Can't Sleep**

1. **light** =

   A **light** helps you see.   Write and spell it: _____

   night = **Night** rhymes with **light**.
   I can't see well at **night**.

   Write and spell it: _____

   right = **Right** rhymes with **light**.
   Do you bat with your **right** hand?

   Write and spell it: _____

2. **new** = **New** rhymes with 2.

   I have a **new** pet.   Write and spell it: _____

3. **like** = **Like** rhymes with

   I **like** to play ball.   Write and spell it: _____

   liked = **like** + t
   The dog **liked** his new tag.

   Write and spell it: _____

4. **window** =

   If the **window** is open, bugs will come in.

   Write and spell it: _____

5. **about** =u + b + out

   This book is **about** trucks.

   Write and spell it: _____

Now read the word list again.

Words for **Greg Can't Sleep**

• Draw a line from each sentence to the picture it goes with.

Do you **like** my **new** pants?

Nan **liked** to swim a lot.

Hal runs to the **window**.

It is **about** ten o'clock.

The **light** is a big help at **night**.

I will be **right** back with your milk!

Greg Can't Sleep

"Why do I have to go to bed now, Mom? I do not feel a bit like sleep. Can't I just stay up till ten?" Greg asks. Greg *never* wants to go to bed, but he can't tell Mom and Dad why. So he just begs to stay up and look at TV.

"But, Dad, can't I stay up? Just this one night?" Greg begs. "Lots of kids in my class do." But Mom and Dad do not give in.

At last Greg gives up and clomps up to bed. Mom comes up and gives him a hug and kiss. Then she snaps off the light.

Ooo! It is so black with no light! Greg gets under his quilt, but then he feels hot so he dumps the quilt off.

Tap! Tap! What is it? Tap, tap, tap! Greg plugs his ears, but he still hears it. "What can it be? Can it be the big, bad wolf? (But a wolf will be after pigs, not kids!) Is it a bad man, a rob•ber? Is he after my new mitt? (But I hid my mitt in the old trunk.) Can it be a bat? (I can't stand bats!) I'll bet it's a mon•ster that wants to get in!" Greg blinks and gulps. "I'll call Mom for a drink," he plans.

"Mom, can you come up?" Greg calls.

Mom comes back and asks Greg what's up. Can she help him?

"I want a glass of milk," he fibs, so Mom gets it. (But then he must drink it. Oh no!)

Then Mom gets up to go.

"I feel a gust of wind. Can you see if the window is up?" Greg asks. Mom looks blank, for she sees the window is down.

"Go to sleep," she says, as she pulls the door so it's open just a crack.

Now the tap, tap, tap begins all over. Greg gets under the bed. (But it's so full of dust it makes him pant and gasp!) So Greg yells, "Dad, I didn't floss!"

"You can do it the next day," Dad grunts.

But Greg can bluff no more. He begins to fuss and rant.

"Mom . . . Dad, a mon•ster is in my room!" he yells. "Come quick!"

So Mom tromps back up the steps to Greg's room.

"Greg, get a grip! It's OK. You can come out from under the bed," Mom hints. "I see *no* mon•sters in this room."

But Greg just rants on. "It's at the window. Hear the tap, tap, tap?"

Mom looks and sees a big, black bug as it hits the glass. "It's a bug. It sees the light from the hall and wants to get in. This bug likes light. Let's put on the lamp so you can see," Mom adds. "Will a light be all right with you?" she asks Greg.

Greg grins and nods. "A light will help . . . the bug, that is."

The next day Mom says, "Do you know what to do if a bug is a pest? You can tick like the clock . . . one, two, one, two, till you go to sleep. You can hum a bit. Or you can hit the bed with your fist and yell, 'I'm brave!' And you know what? You *will* be brave!"

"My mom knows a lot about bugs and kids and all kinds of stuff," Greg says to him•self. "But, best of all, she knows a lot about me!"

Yes **No** **Can't Tell**

- Draw the face to show the answer.

1. Did Greg go to bed after ten o'clock?

2. Did Greg tell Mom and Dad why he didn't
   want to go to bed?

3. Did Dad and Mom make Greg go to bed?

4. Was Greg sick of his bed·room?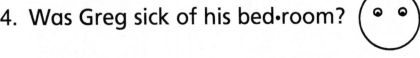

5. Did Greg see a bat at the window?

6. Did milk help put Greg to sleep?

7. Did Greg feel bad with the light off?

Tell what you can do if the room is black and you hear a tap.

_____

- -

_____

Draw what was at the window and how Greg looks as he hears the tap.

Think About It!

1. Name a thing that can tap that is not a bug.

_____

- -

_____

2. How are the sun and a lamp alike?

_____

- -

_____

3. What will hap·pen if you run with a glass of milk in your hand?

_____

- -

_____

4. How are a window and a door alike?

_____

- -

_____

5. Tell what you can drink that is hot.

_____

- -

_____

6. Why did Mom ask if it was OK to put on the light?

_____

- -

_____

Can You Figure This Out?

• Write an answer to each question.

What can you:

jump on? _____

    see at night? _____

       find in the grass? _____

          make by your·self? _____

What can you open? _____

    What can you hear? _____

      What do you want to do some·day? _____

Introduction to **Max**

• Draw a line from the word to the picture of the word.
Some of the words are review words from *Beyond the Code 1*.

book   hair

told   feet

cold   two

ear

Which Words Rhyme?

• Draw a line from the word in the first list to the word that rhymes
in the second list.

scamp	skip
scold	why
look	old
flip	stamp
scrub	took
try	tub

Words for **Max**

1. **only** = O + n + L + E

   I am **only** six.   Write and spell it: _____

2. **care** = **Care** rhymes with **bear**.

   If I go away, will you take **care** of my pet rat?

   Write and spell it: _____

3. **head** = hed

   She nods her **head**.   Write and spell it: _____

4. **cool** = **Cool** rhymes with .

   The wind is **cool**.   Write and spell it: _____

5. **snow** = sn + O (**Snow** rhymes with **grow**.)

   Snow fell to•day.   Write and spell it: _____

6. **spaghetti** = spu + get + E

   Do you like to eat **spaghetti**?

   Write and spell it: _____

7. **said** = sed

   Did you hear what I **said**?

   Write and spell it: _____

Now read the word list again.

Words for **Max**

• Draw a line from each sentence to the picture it goes with.

I have **only** one pet.

I do not **care** if it **snows**.

He makes a big pot of **spaghetti**.

A bug is on your **head**.

Liz **said,** "Bats are **cool!"**

Max

Max was only two, but he was on the go! Max liked to skip and play in the grass. He liked to hop and jump and do flips. He liked to run and play ball with his dog. But, best of all, Max liked to make a big mess.

Max was only two, but his Mom and Dad said, "What can we do? Max likes to mess in mud and muck and stuff. And that is not at all good to do."

But Max did not care; he was only two!

Max liked to put sand on his head. He let it run down his neck and it got in his hair. Max did not care if it got in his ears. He did not care if it got in his bed.

"It's fun!" was all Max said.

Max just had a ball! He did not care at all!

One day Max was out with his dog, Rags. He took some grass and put it on his head. Then he put grass on his dog's head.

"This is fun," Max said. "I'll pull up lots of grass and put it all over my head. I like the feel of grass on my feet," he said, "but, best of all, I like grass on my head."

Mom said Max must get in the tub and rub and scrub. But Max didn't care if he was a mess.

"I like to sit in the tub!" he said.

The next day Max saw a lump of mud.

"Ooo! Cool!" Max said. Slop, slop, slop! "I'll put some on my head. It will feel so cool."

The mud ran down and got in his ears, and his hair was all wet as well. But did Max care? Not one bit!

Mom said Max was a mess! Dad said Max must go to bed!

"OK, I'll go," Max said.

Max was not glum or mad, for what he did was not at all bad.

Then one day snow falls, and it is so cold. Max likes to play in the snow a lot. He packs a snow·ball and gives it a toss. His dog, Rags, runs to get it, but it's lost.

"No, Rags, it's not a ball! It's just snow!" Max calls.

Then Max pulls off his hat and puts snow on his head.

"Look, I'm a snow·man!" is what Max said.

You can bet that Max was cold, but he didn't care. Dad said he must be a po·lar bear!

It's six o'clock as Max sits down to eat. Dad has put on a big pot of spaghetti.

"I like spaghetti," Max says. "It's so good!"

Max eats a lot and then asks for more. Do you know what hap·pens next? Max pops it right on top of his head . . . and rubs and rubs till his head is all red.

Now Max's Mom just wags her head.

"Ooo! What can we do with this kid? Why must he make a big mess? What can we do so he'll stop? What will he want to do next? What, oh, what can we do?"

Can you tell Mom and Dad what to do?

Yes 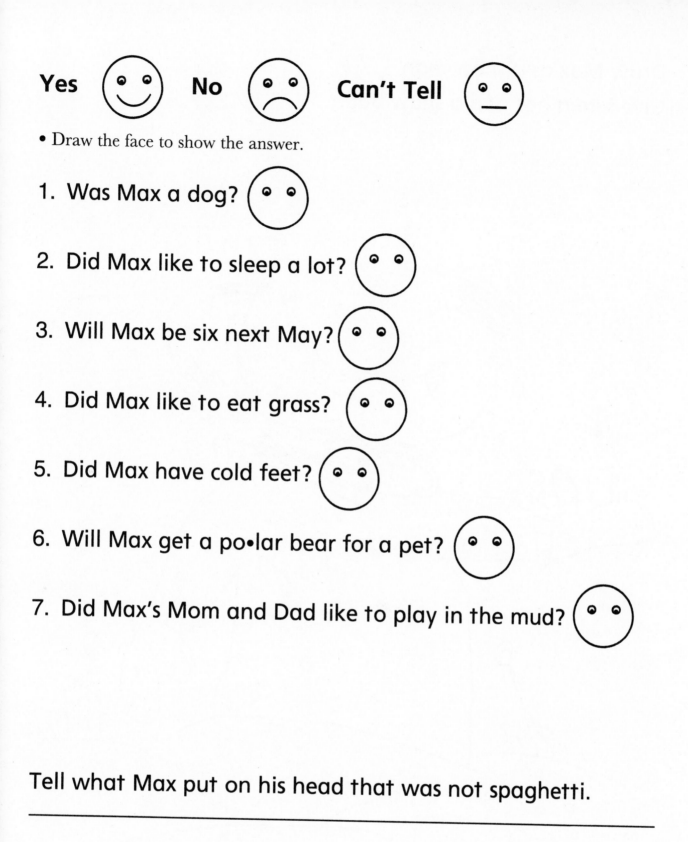 **No** **Can't Tell**

• Draw the face to show the answer.

1. Was Max a dog?

2. Did Max like to sleep a lot?

3. Will Max be six next May?

4. Did Max like to eat grass?

5. Did Max have cold feet?

6. Will Max get a po•lar bear for a pet?

7. Did Max's Mom and Dad like to play in the mud?

Tell what Max put on his head that was not spaghetti.

_____

- -

_____

Draw Max as a snow·man.
Give him a hat and a snow·ball.

Think About It!

1. Name one thing you can step in that is not mud.

2. Tell what you can pull that is not hair.

3. Name a ball that is not a snow·ball.

4. Why did Max like to put things on his head?

5. Why didn't Max care if he was a mess?

6. What can Mom and Dad do about Max?

Can You Figure This Out?

• Circle the word on each line that does not fit.

1. night   sun•up   dusk   day   tricks

2. look   see   pond   wink   blink

3. slip   fall   trip   bump   belt

4. bear   fox   plump   wolf   skunk

5. cry   sniff   sob   yell   plants

6. snow•man   hat   swim   sled   mit•tens

7. hot dogs   bricks   nuts   spaghetti   mints

Words for **Good, Bad, or Best?**

1. **could** = **Could** rhymes with **good**.

   I **could** not sleep.   Write and spell it: _____

   would = **Would** rhymes with **could**.

   I **would** like to fly.    Write and spell it: _____

2. **were** = **Were** rhymes with **her**.

   They **were** glad to have a flag.

   Write and spell it: _____

3. **talk** =

   Tim and Sal **talk** a lot.   Write and spell it: _____

   walk = **Walk** rhymes with **talk**.

   She likes to **walk** in the mud.

   Write and spell it: _____

4. **over** = O + ver

   Lin runs **over** to see her pal.

   Write and spell it: _____

5. **also** = all + so

   She plays golf and **also** swims well.

   Write and spell it: _____

Now read the word list again.

Words for **Good, Bad, or Best?**

- Draw a line from each sentence to the picture it goes with.

Al **could** not lift it.

Would you **also** like a lick?

Kit and Nick took a **walk** and had a **talk**.

They held hands, for they **were** best pals.

Meg jumps **over** Griff.

Good, Bad, or Best?

As a pup Fred was the *best* pet ever, but now and then he was so *bad*. He could be a pest and play pranks as fast as you can blink! But he could also do all kinds of tricks! He could sit up and yip, roll over and grin. What a cool dog!

But Fred could be a scamp. He'd jump up on beds, step on books, pull plugs, tip over the clock, and bump the lamp off the desk. If you had a glass of milk in your hand, Fred would bump into you and you'd spill it. Or he'd run into the room, tip over a box full of crisp snacks, and then run off with them! Fred was full of all kinds of pranks.

We said Fred must have felt bad. All we did was yell at him. Still, the next day he'd be back at his pranks. (If Fred felt bad, we could *not* tell!)

But Mom was strict. "Fred, you can't act like this," Mom said. "You must go to dog class so you will grow up to be a well-bred dog." So off Fred went to class, but he did not pass. He was the *only* pup to flunk *all* the tests. What a scamp!

One day I said to Mom, "I'll have a talk with Fred. He's a good dog and he must want to do well."

So I held on to Fred and said, "Sit, Fred!" Fred had a look that said, "Let's play," but he sat down.

"Look, Fred, this can't go on! I know you want to have fun, but you must stop your pranks. Let's have no more, do you hear? Or Mom says you'll have to go a•way for good!"

Fred's ears went up fast. What was that you said? *"For good?"*

Fred *was* sad. He felt so bad that we were all mad.
In the past he was a scamp, but he was just a pup then.
Fred didn't want to be bad now, but he didn't know the
right way to act.

"I'd best get with it and try to be good. I can see that
I must grow up at last," Fred said. "I'll try to be good.
I'll try my best!"

Now Fred is a grand dog, fun to be with, so good and so kind. And just look at his new tricks! He can twist and flip and stand on his back legs. We clap and clap and call him the best dog. We hug him and pat him and give him a snack.

Fred must have felt bad to act as he had. But I ask you, can we now trust this pup who was so bad? Do we have a new Fred or is it just an act to get us off his back?

"*Ruff, ruff!*"

What was that you said, Fred?

Yes 🙂 **No** ☹️ **Can't Tell** 😐

- Draw the face to show the answer.

1. Did Fred like to drink milk? 😐

2. Was Fred ever a pest? 😐

3. Did Fred pass his dog class? 😐

4. Could Fred grin? 😐

5. Did Fred feel bad that they were all mad at him? 😐

6. Did Fred know how to act right? 😐

7. Is Fred a well-bred dog now? 😐

Tell one bad thing that Fred did.

_____

- -

_____

Draw more of Fred as he stands on his back legs to get a snack.

Think About It!

1. What can you dump out that is not snacks?

_____

_____

2. Name two things you can flip.

_____

_____

3. How are a dog and a fox alike?

_____

_____

4. Name a thing you can·not hold in your hand.

_____

_____

5. What would you say to your dog if you scold him?

_____

_____

6. What did Fred do to be·come "the best pet"?

_____

_____

Can You Figure This Out?

• Finish each sentence with a word that fits.
The first letter of the word is written for you.

1. A lid snaps; a door S_____.

2. You hit a drum; you kick a b_____.

3. You can eat a plum; you can drink m_____.

4. A cab·in has a door; a tent has a f_____.

5. You put a hat on your head; you put socks on your
f_____.

6. On a green light you go; on a red light you S_____.

7. You go down a river on a raft; you go down a snow·bank
on a S_____.

8. You fill a sack; you pack a b_____.

Words for **Stand up for Lemonade**

1. **bored** = b + or + d
   If I am **bored** I do not know what to do.

   Write and spell it: _____

2. **street** = ![street] (**Street** rhymes with **feet**.)
   We look as we cross the **street**.

   Write and spell it: _____

3. **lemonade** = lem + un + A + d
   Lemonade is a good drink.

   Write and spell it: _____

4. **money** = mun + E
   I have no **money** to spend.   Write and spell it: _____

5. **people** = p + E + pl
   Can all the **people** fit in the van?

   Write and spell it: _____

6. **wagon** = wag + en
   I have a new red **wagon**.

   Write and spell it: _____

7. **soccer** = sock + er
   It's fun to play **soccer**.

   Write and spell it: _____

Now read the word list again.

Words for **Stand up for Lemonade**

• Draw a line from each sentence to the picture it goes with.

I am **bored** with TV.

I like to pull my **wagon**.

Ron drinks **lemonade** on a hot day.

He must not play **soccer** in the **street**.

Min has **money** to get a new ball.

People say he plays so well.

Stand up for Lemonade

"It's so hot, and I'm bored," says Hank. "Do you want to go for a swim or jog to the pond and skip rocks?" he asks Ann, his twin.

Ann nods. "OK. But would it be more fun to set up a stand and sell lemonade? We could get 50¢ for a big cup and 25¢ for a small cup. Do you want to do that? Wouldn't it be fun?"

"Let me see, I could get a new soccer ball with the money I make," plans Hank. "OK. You win! Let's sell lemonade."

So the twins make a list of what they must get to set up the stand. They find a big box to put the cups on. Next, Ann gets her new bank to keep the money in. Then Dad helps the kids make pink lemonade.

"Let's sell crisp snacks as well," adds Hank. (He wants to make lots of money!)

Last of all, they cut up an old dress for a flag and with a pen they print the cost of the drinks and snacks. Then they put the flag on a stick. The kids have lots of stuff now! So they cram it in a wag·on and set off to look for a good spot to sell drinks.

The kids lug the wagon up West Street and dump the stuff in front of Mr. Sam's. Ann asks if they can set up the stand. Mr. Sam says it's OK, but they must pick up well at the end of the day.

"I do not want a bit of junk left on my door•step," he tells her.

Now the twins get all set up to sell, but *no* luck! No one walks by! Some trucks come by but do not stop. At last a van putts up the hill and stops right in front of the stand.

"Hi!" puffs the van man.

"Want a drink?" asks Hank.

"Hand it to me!" yells the man in the van. Ann fills the cup to the rim and gives it to him.

"Send me the bill!" yells the van man, and then he's off. What bad luck! The kids are mad that they had trust in that man!

The day drags on, but still they do not sell. Hank swats bugs, and Ann hums rock and roll. They are so bored.

At last a pick-up truck limps up with a flat. A gal gets out. "Fill her up! I'll have a big lemonade," she says and sits down. She must rest till she can get help with the flat, so she spends some more on snacks.

In a bit her pal Deb stops to help. Deb has a cool drink and tells the kids it's swell.

It's so, so hot . . . and so the twins have a swig or two as well.

At last more people stop by till no drinks or snacks are left. Ann sends Hank back for more stuff, but Dad says it's six o'clock and best to pack up.

That night the twins are in bliss, for they have $10.50 to split!

"It was the best day! You've got to hand it to me!" brags Ann. "A lemonade stand was a grand plan!"

Hank nods and grins. "But on the next hot day let's go for a swim!"

Yes 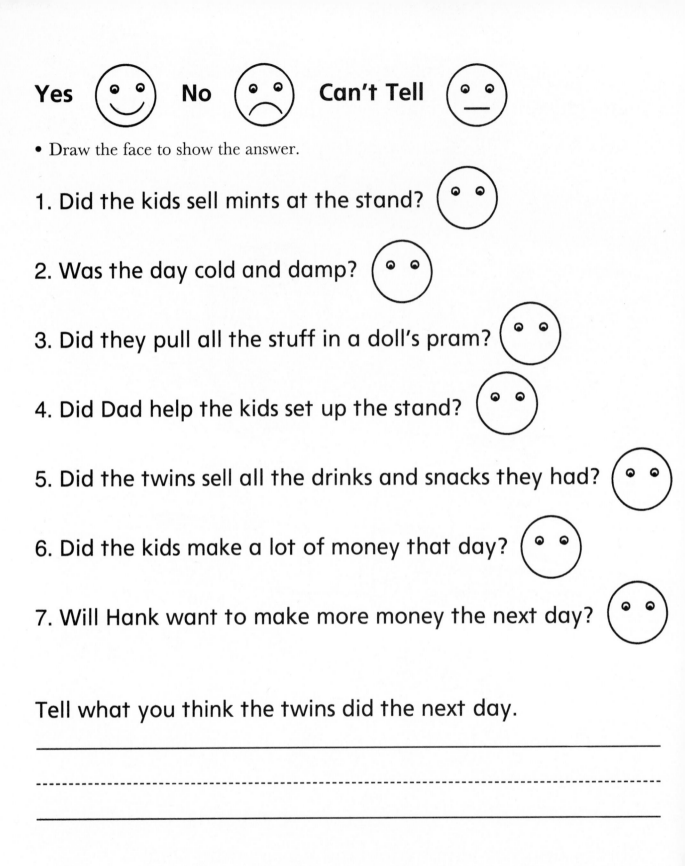 **No** **Can't Tell**

• Draw the face to show the answer.

1. Did the kids sell mints at the stand?

2. Was the day cold and damp?

3. Did they pull all the stuff in a doll's pram?

4. Did Dad help the kids set up the stand?

5. Did the twins sell all the drinks and snacks they had?

6. Did the kids make a lot of money that day?

7. Will Hank want to make more money the next day?

Tell what you think the twins did the next day.

_____

_____

_____

_____

_____

Draw more of the wagon. Add some cups and the flag.

Think About It!

1. Name two things you can drink that are not lemonade.

_____

_____

2. Tell one thing you can put money in.

_____

_____

3. Why did the twins have to pack up at six o'clock?

_____

_____

4. What can you do if you are bored?

_____

_____

5. How are a cup and a glass alike?

_____

_____

6. The twins set up a lemonade stand. What else can
   stand mean?

_____

_____

Can You Figure This Out?

• Find the word on the bug that is the best answer
and write it on the line.

1. What can you pull stuff in? _____

2. What means a gulp or two? _____

3. What do you do at a red light? _____

4. What can you put your money in? _____

5. What helps you see at night? _____

6. What grows in the sun on the window·sill? _____

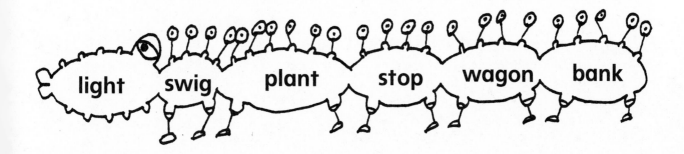

light   swig   plant   stop   wagon   bank

Introduction to **Lost in the City**

• Sometimes two words are put together to make a new word. Put the two small words together to make the bigger word. Then read all the words after the equals sign.

1. with + out = without socks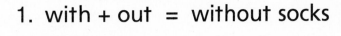

2. my + self = all by myself

3. sub + way = subway stop

4. book + store = at the bookstore

5. for + get = forget about the test

6. a + head = go ahead of me

7. up + set = upset at the sad news

Words for **Lost in the City**

1. **store** = (**Store** rhymes with **more**.)
   We went to the **store** to get a ball.

   Write and spell it: _____

2. **climb** = cl + I + m
   It's fun to **climb** a tree.

   Write and spell it: _____

3. **build** = bild
   I like to **build** with blocks.

   Write and spell it: _____

   building = build + ing
   I live in a tall **building**.

   Write and spell it: _____

4. **city** = sit + E
   A **city** has lots of buildings.

   Write and spell it: _____

5. **playground** =
   It's fun to go to the **playground**.

   Write and spell it: _____

6. **don't** = d + O + nt
   I **don't** like the smell of skunks.

   Write and spell it: _____

Now read the word list again.

Words for **Lost in the City**

• Draw a line from each sentence to the picture it goes with.

Jill plays with a pal at the **playground**.

It's fun to **build** a fire.

Lots of people live in the **city**.

Cal will get ham at the **store**.

I **don't** know if Don can **climb** the steps.

Can Rob fix up the old **building**?

Lost in the City

It's fun to live in the city. I am never bored. I can walk down the street and get a snack or go to the book•store or take the sub•way to the rink. (I never go with•out Mom or Dad.) Best of all, I like to go to the playground next to my building. (I can go all by my•self.)

My pal Kim also likes this playground. Kim has red hair and is in my class at PS 109. She likes to play soccer and climb trees, just like I do. We have lots of fun. Kim is my best pal.

To·day as I come to the playground, Kim runs over and asks, "Do you want to help me build in the sand?"

"That'll be fun," I tell her. We play in the sand and talk about what we saw on TV last night.

"Let's climb to the top of the Look Out," I yell to Kim. At the top we stick our heads out and look down. What fun to be up by the tops of the trees! We stand and talk. I tell Kim I have a new book about rats. Kim likes rats and so do I.

Now Kim sees the new Red Sox hat I just got from Dad. She tells me it's the best ever! (Kim is a Red Sox fan.) But she has a Cubs ball cap on! (Her mom is a Cubs fan.)

"Do you want to swap hats for a day?" I ask.

"Let's!" she gasps. "Will your Dad care if we swap?" I just grin and wag my head.

"Is it after 4 P.M. yet?" Kim asks at last as she looks for a clock. "I have to go. Mom wants me back by 4:30. Want to walk with me? It's only a block or two," she adds.

"Why not?" I tell her. ("Will Mom find out?" I ask my·self. She has told me never to go by my·self, but it's just a block or two.)

We walk down the street and look in the store windows. "Let's stop and get a snack," I tell Kim as we pass a hot dog stand. "I've got some money we can spend." So we get a hot dog and a bag of nuts to split.

We skip down the street, go to the right, and come to a tall, brick building.

"This is where I live," Kim says. "But I have to go now. It's after 4:30. Bye, Tess! See you in class!" Kim skips in the door fast.

As the door slams, I blink. I don't know where I am or what streets I took. I look blank. I don't know what to do. Do I go left or right? What can I do?

A bus full of people hums by. Then, SCREEEEEEE!
A fire truck zips down the street. I walk on, and I don't
look up till I bump into an old man. He tips his hat at
me, but I can't ask him for help. My dad has told me
never to talk to people I don't know. As I cross the street
I for·get to look at the light, and a taxi honks at me. I
blink and stop fast! Lots of people walk by, but no one I
know! Am I lost?

My head begins to spin and I feel sick, so I slip into a store to rest a bit. I tell my·self not to cry. If I look up and down the street I may get a hint of where to go, but it all looks so odd. Now I know I'm LOST!

I begin to cry. Will I ever get back? I can't yell for help. I can't grab a cab or make a call, for I've spent all my money. WAAA! But I can't have a spaz! I must get a grip!

I drift down the street and try to act cool. "I'll find my way!" I sniff. I hunt up and down the street for a store I know. Then up ahead I see a store that looks just like Mr. Zeb's. Can it be?

"Hi, Mr. Zeb," I call as I run by. Now I see my bus stop . . . and down the street is where I live!

I did find it, all by my·self!

Just then I run into my mom! She is on her way back from her job. She has had a bad day, but she's glad to see me.

"Where have you been?" Mom asks.

"Just out for a spin," I gasp as I run up to my room. I can't let Mom know I got lost. She's told me never to go out by my•self. I did have Kim with me . . . for a bit! But from now on I'll do as Mom says.

Yes **No** **Can't Tell**

• Draw the face to show the answer.

1. Do Tess and her pal Kim like to go to the playground?

2. Did Kim go to the playground by her·self?

3. Did the two pals live ten blocks away?

4. Did Tess have a book about cats?

5. Did Dad care if Kim took the Red Sox cap for a night?

6. Did lots of people help Tess find her way back?

7. Did Mr. Zeb run a pet store?

How do you feel if you are lost and can't find your way?

_____

- -

_____

Draw the rest of the man and the city. Add a stop•light.

Think About It!

1. Name two things you can climb to the top of.

   _____

   _____

   _____

2. Name two things you can see on a city street.

   _____

   _____

   _____

3. Why did Tess feel sick and her head begin to spin?

   _____

   _____

   _____

4. Why did Dad tell Tess not to talk to people she didn't know?

   _____

   _____

   _____

5. How are a bus and a truck alike?

   _____

   _____

   _____

6. Tell what you would do if you were lost.

   _____

   _____

   _____

Can You Figure This Out?

• Circle the word on each line that does not fit.

1. bus   truck   wagon   help   van

2. jump   walk   sleep   skip   climb

3. milk   camp   so·da   tea   lemonade

4. flag   build   make   blend   mix

5. store   skip   mall   tent   building

6. grin   street   ramp   track   dock

7. playground   rink   bank   skin   hall

Words Introduced in *Beyond The Code 2*

about	hear	right
after	kind	roll
also	know	said
bear	lemonade	snow
bored	light	soccer
build	like	spaghetti
building	liked	store
care	make	street
city	money	take
climb	never	talk
cool	new	that
could	night	wagon
don't	now	walk
ever	only	want
find	over	were
fire	people	window
grow	playground	would